TEXT AND ILLUS... P9-CRT-167

JAMES F. KLAWITER

REST
STOP

CPH
SAINT LOUIS®

*Devotions for
the Road of Life*

Scripture quotations, unless otherwise indicated, are taken from the HOLY BIBLE,
NEW INTERNATIONAL VERSION ®. NIV ® . Copyright © 1973, 1978, 1984 by International Bible Society.
Used by permission of Zondervan Publishing House. All rights reserved.

Scripture quotations marked KJV are from the King James or Authorized Version of the Bible.

Hymn verse on page 56 taken from *Lutheran Worship,*
Copyright © 1982 by Concordia Publishing House.

Text and internal art copyright © 2001 James F. Klawiter

Cover illustration by Reggie Holladay

Published by Concordia Publishing House
3558 S. Jefferson Avenue, St. Louis, MO 63118-3968
Manufactured in the United States of America

Library of Congress Cataloging-in-Publication Data

Klawiter, James F.
    Rest stop:devotions for the road of life/James F. Klawiter, author and illustrator.
        p. cm.
    ISBN 0-570-05269-6
    1. Devotional literature.   I. Title.
BV4832.2 .K555 2001
242--dc21   2001001368

1   2   3   4   5   6   7   8   9   10   10 09 08 07 06 05 04 03 02 01

Contents...

Let's Go...

Rest Stop

"Come to Me, all you who are weary and burdened, and I will give you rest." Matthew 11:28

One of the blessings of the interstate highway system is the rest stop. I believe it was the invention of a highway planner who had traveled with kids in the back seat. Rest stops seem to appear every 50 miles or so, just long enough for bladders to fill and backsides to become numb. The blue sign with the message, "Rest Stop 2 Miles" is always a welcomed sight.

What a relief to get out of the car and stretch those legs with a stroll to the facilities. A short nap can be even more comforting. Indeed, the rest stop is a blessing for all who travel the interstate.

But on the interstates of life, where are the rest stops? Home used to be, but traffic has increased. Television, the Internet, and our racing schedules have turned our homes into drive-ins and drive-outs. Not much time for rest.

Even churches are affected by our on-the-go lifestyles. Instead of viewing church as a place to receive the gifts of grace our Lord offers, many who attend worship are only concerned about self-gratification. In response, many churches are trying to

find the most efficient and entertaining form of worship. Many times this effort to streamline church services becomes the primary focus of the congregation instead of praising and thanking our loving and almighty God.

The only real rest stop in life is Jesus Christ. We provide weary, burdened souls; He provides the rest. In Jesus we find forgiveness for all of our past "driving" violations. In Him we find the water and bread of life that revives us. In Him we also find how to get to our eternal destination: "I am the Way and the Truth and the Life. No one comes to the Father except through Me" (John 14:6).

Jesus doesn't appear just every 50 miles or so or just once a week. He is always available to give you rest. He tells us so in the Bible. You can always reach Him with all of your joys and concerns through prayer.

God, in His perfect planning, engineered a perfect Rest Stop for us—His Son, Jesus Christ. Get off life's interstate and rest a while.

Prayer

Thank You, Lord Jesus, for providing us a place of rest, both physical and spiritual. We thank You for giving Your life for our sins and showing us the way to eternal rest. Bless us on our way with Your presence and direction. In Your name we pray. Amen.

For further reading ... Luke 24:13–35

Car Pools

Let us not give up meeting together, as some are in the habit of doing, but let us encourage one another—and all the more as you see the Day approaching. Hebrews 10:25

One of the many devices cities use to cut down on traffic, especially during morning and evening drive times, is the car pool. The idea is to get individual commuters into a car or van with other commuters to decrease congestion, pollution, and expense. Although carpooling is growing in popularity, it's still not difficult to find an abundance of vehicles with only one occupant during rush hour.

In addition, it seems that many have expanded the adage "my home is my castle" to "my car is my mobile castle." We can shut out the world, crank up the radio, turn on the A/C, and be the independent monarch of our own shiny travel capsule. Many of us are reluctant to give up this travel independence by joining a car pool.

This is similar to what happens to church members. It doesn't take many incidents, aided by the promptings of Satan, to convince the church-goer that getting up for church every Sunday is a pain. Sundays are for rest and relaxation, and that does not logically include spending an entire morning in

Sunday school and worship. Instead, many people watch a slick, televised church show in the comfort of their own homes. Others feel they can worship God quite effectively from their bass boats and lake cottages.

But God is one jump ahead of us. He knows what we're thinking. He inspired the writer of Hebrews to remind us, "Let us not give up meeting together, as some are in the habit of doing." Skipping church is not a recent development. The only difference between today and the time Hebrews was written is that today we probably have more excuses.

But God doesn't want us to skip divine services. He doesn't want us to pass up opportunities to worship. God wants us to join a spiritual car pool. He wants us to travel the road of life with our fellow saints. Hebrews continues, "But let us encourage one another." When we are in church singing, praying, listening, or communing, other Christian travelers are encouraged in their faith development. You can't encourage fellow Christians by watching church on TV or by sitting with a fishing pole in the middle of a lake.

Remember, Christ our Lord gave up His peace and quiet in heaven and joined your crowded and confining car pool. He even endured the ultimate head-on collision with sin as He suffered and died on the cross for us. Jesus' resurrection from the dead promises that all who believe in Him will one day inherit a mansion in heaven. There, our car pools will be eternal journeys with our fellow-redeemed.

Maybe that's why this text ends with the thought, "and all the more as you see the Day approaching." That "Day" is the day Christ comes. When He comes, we can trust that He will have already made room for us in His car pool.

Prayer

Dear Savior, lead us away from ourselves and our personal wants to join You and our fellow-redeemed as we travel together into eternity. We pray according to Your will. Amen.

For further reading ... 1 Corinthians 12:12–26

Reading Maps

"I am the Way and the Truth and the Life. No one comes to the Father except through Me." John 14:6

The disciple Thomas states the truth that so many male drivers never dare to utter, "Lord, we don't know where You are going, *so how can we know the way?*" (John 14:5). I wonder how many men would admit this same thought to their wives, "Dear, I don't know how to get there."

Some say this is a "guy thing;" never asking for directions and never admitting being lost. But it isn't just a "guy thing." It's a people thing.

Although many people believe that men have cornered the market on refusing to ask for directions, the truth is that we all have a hard time admitting when we're lost.

Built into the human nature is something called pride. Pride keeps someone from asking directions. Pride is what the serpent used to pry Adam and Eve away from the direction God had given them. And pride is what keeps all of us from admitting our weaknesses and shortcomings.

Pride can also lead us to reject our human need for divine intervention in eternal salvation. No matter how often we hear the Good News that Jesus paid our way into the eternal banquet, we are inclined to want to leave a tip. We foolishly want to add our own effort to insure our salvation a little more. God's complete package of grace, grasped by faith and nurtured by Word and Sacrament, can be difficult for our sinful pride to accept.

Therefore Jesus' answer to all the lost Thomases provides a map, especially for those who think they don't need one. Jesus said, "I am the Way and the Truth and the Life. No one comes to the Father except through Me."

Jesus is the only route to heaven. But how many spiritual motorists, after hearing and seeing this route marked out in the red of His blood, still insist on finding their own way? Some choose to build their own road, paving it with good works. Some fill themselves with 110 octane emotionalism, hoping to blast their way in. Still others are spiritual engineers who, with knowledge and ancient philosophic maps, plan a new way to the Father. Some even invent a new father.

God clearly gives us the *only* Map to salvation and eternal life—His Son Jesus Christ.

Jesus blazed the trail, destroyed the roadblocks, created paths through the dead ends, and finally gave Himself in death to be our only Bridge to an eternal destination with the Father. And now we read the words of our risen Savior, "I am the Way and the Truth and the Life. No one comes to the Father except through Me."

How about that? Not only a map (Truth) and a road (Way), but free gas (Life). When God maps out a route, He does it right.

Prayer

Dear Lord God, our heavenly Guide, keep us on the route You have laid out for us. Supply us with the strength needed to complete each day's journey. Enable us to help our fellow travelers as You lead us to Your kingdom in heaven. We ask these things in the name of Your Son who bought our salvation in full. Amen.

For further reading ... John 4:4–42

The DMV

**We must all appear before the judgment seat of Christ, that each one may receive what is due him for the things done while in the body, whether good or bad.
2 Corinthians 5:10**

No matter where you live there is a name for it. In California it is called the Department of Motor Vehicles, or the DMV. For all drivers, unless one works there, it can be a most disturbing place.

The Department of Motor Vehicles is a place of standing and waiting. It is a place of confusing directions and lengthy forms. It is a place of driving tests and written tests. It is also a place that will give your checkbook plenty of exercise. The Department of Motor Vehicles forces people to take legal responsibility for their vehicles and for their driving. In short, the DMV is a place most of us try to avoid.

St. Paul reminds us that there is a place where we will be forced to take responsibility for our actions in the journey of life. Paul writes, "We must *all* appear." There will be no delays, no excuses, and no postponements on the Last Day. All people will appear before Jesus Christ. Instead of a driving record, each person will be confronted with their "living record."

Paul continues, "that each one may receive what is due him for the things done while in the body, whether good or bad."

If we would read no further, this last visit to Jesus' DMV would indeed be our worst nightmare. Every one of us has black marks on our living record. We are all sinners, no matter how hard we try to do what is right. If God gave salvation only to those who lived perfect lives, we would all be in a lot of trouble.

But we exclaim, "What about our faith in Jesus as our only Savior from sin? What about our claiming His blood as the payment for our sin?"

Put yourself in the scene at the end of time. No one will have trouble knowing who Jesus is. The time of faith will end when our eyes finally see Him in the flesh. All people will be forced to acknowledge Jesus Christ as Lord and Savior. Everyone will see Jesus and know that He has returned to take all believers to heaven. But the opportunity to know Him by faith will have passed. There will be many who will call out, "Lord! Lord." But as recorded in Matthew 7:23 (KJV), Jesus will reply, "I never knew you!"

On what basis will Jesus the Eternal Judge render His judgment? An earthly judge would render judgment according to the letter of the law. But Christ will judge according to the promise of grace—whether we have received His gift in faith or rejected it. Good works are simply evidence of our faith through the saving blood of Jesus Christ.

Therefore, we can look forward to our moment before the Judge with joyful anticipation. Jesus is our Savior. The Holy Spirit has planted faith in Jesus in our hearts at our Baptism and continues to strengthen us. That last great Day may be a DMV (Dreaded Moment Venue) for unbelievers, but for us it will truly be an MDV (Most Desired Victory).

Prayer

Thank You, dear Jesus, for assuring us of our passing from death to life through the power of Your redemption. Thank You for using me to reflect Your grace and glory to all those around me. In Your holy name. Amen.

For further reading ... 1 Thessalonians 4:13–18

Slow Trucks

"Which of these three do you think was a neighbor to the man who fell into the hands of robbers?" The expert in the law replied, "The one who had mercy on him." Jesus told him, "Go and do likewise." Luke 10:36–37

Almost everyone has heard the parable of the Good Samaritan. Jesus uses this story to teach people that everyone is their neighbor. Christians are to help anyone who is in need—to be on the lookout for robbed and beaten travelers. And more practically, we can look for opportunities to help those who have everyday needs: a neighbor who needs a ride, a solicitor for a worthy charity, or a volunteer for the annual food drive.

These neighbors are fairly easy to identify. However, there are other neighbors in need who aren't so easy to identify. Think about the last time you were on a winding, two-lane road behind a slow truck. Perhaps it methodically tried to grind its way up a steep grade, getting slower and slower by the minute. Recall your thoughts. They probably weren't too complimentary toward the truck, its driver, or the highway department that should have put in a passing lane.

What can you as a neighbor do for the slow truck? Pulling out every two minutes to see if you can pass isn't much help. Laying on the horn and flashing your lights doesn't offer any particular encouragement or comfort. How about backing off a car length or two? Maybe putting on your emergency flashers to alert other drivers. You might even offer a prayer for the almost stalled-out truck driver. A slow truck, a slow train, or a slow anybody doesn't need our foot-tapping—but rather our empathy and patience.

The irony is that we have all been that slow, nearly stalled-out truck. We were all loaded down with sin and death until Jesus came along. Without Jesus' undeserved patience, love, and grace, none of us would ever make it up the hill to salvation. Instead of honking at us or gesturing out the window, Jesus came to our aid and towed us and our sins to the cross. Because of Jesus' selfless act, we are now saved and enjoy the promise of eternal life.

In response to Jesus' incredible love, we can identify the slow trucks in our lives and gladly offer kind words, patience, and encouragement.

Prayer

Dear Lord God, help us to be patient with those whom we think impede our progress. We ask You to forgive us for the many times we hold up the progress of Your kingdom on earth through our selfish sins. Give to us Your Holy Spirit who encourages us by strengthening our faith in You. We ask you to hear and bless our requests for Jesus' sake. Amen.

For further reading ... Matthew 25:31–46

Adopt-a-Highway

For you did not receive a spirit that makes you a slave again to fear, but you received the Spirit of Sonship. And by Him we cry, "Abba, Father." Romans 8:15

One of the most pleasant parts of camping is getting acquainted with new people. On one occasion, my wife and I had the pleasure of meeting two families from Germany. As with anyone visiting a foreign country, they had questions. One member of the family asked, "What do those 'Adopt-a-Highway' signs mean?" Such signs do not exist in Germany because their roadways are immaculate. There is no trash to pick up.

We explained that American roadways are, unfortunately, far from clean. States, therefore, organize a program in which various groups, in exchange for their name on a sign, agree to "adopt" a mile of highway and accept responsibility for keeping it litter free.

It isn't so large a leap to see the similarity here in what our heavenly Father did when He adopted us as His own. He paid our adoption fee with the life of His only Son. And the clean-up job is not yet complete. Day after day God's adopted highways (you and me) are littered with the trash called sin. And day after day, God's spirit faithfully picks up the litter and loads it onto the back of Jesus Christ, to be dumped into the enormous landfill called Calvary.

St. Paul expressed this truth when he wrote, "You did not receive a spirit that makes you a slave again to fear." Our adoption as God's children is just that, an adoption. It is not a state of slavery or fearful servitude. We are His adopted children whom He loves unconditionally. Our relationship with Him is characterized by the intimate greeting "Abba, Father!" These words are similar to the first words a child calls out in recognition of "Da-Da." We are able to call God "Daddy" only because His only-begotten Son interceded on our behalf through His death on the cross.

If only we had told those visitors from Germany about God's "Adopt-a-Sinner Program." That really would have amazed them!

Prayer

Abba Father, thank You for adopting us as Your true sons and daughters. Thank You for daily sending Your Spirit to strengthen our faith and encourage us in Your Word. We especially thank You for sending Your Son to buy us back from sin, death, and the devil. In Jesus' name we pray. Amen.

For further reading ... Luke 15:11–32

One Way!

Do not be anxious about anything, but in everything, by prayer and petition, with thanksgiving, present your requests to God.
Philippians 4:6

This verse can be used to combat one of the most universal human defects: worry. Philippians clearly states, "Do not be anxious about anything." This verse goes on to catalog the different ways of communicating with the Lord: prayer, petition, and thanksgiving.

Prayer is the catch-all term for talking to God. Petition includes all of the occasions when we ask God for something. And thanksgiving takes place when we thank and praise God for His goodness. Paul tells us that there is no subject of concern in which God is not interested: "But in everything ... present your requests to God."

Prayer is like a one-way street, an avenue to our heavenly Father. He has promised to hear our joys and concerns and to act according to His rich mercy in Christ.

God's response is a one-way street aimed in our direction. Some may expect God to answer their prayers with dramatic signs from heaven or with a divine whisper in their ear. But that isn't how the Lord works. God comes to us in His Word—read, spoken, and remembered. He also comes to us in the means of grace. If we want to hear what God has to say to us, we read or listen to His Word. If we want to see what God has done for us, we can look to His Sacraments. Baptism is God's action of taking us into His family and forgiving our sins. Holy Communion is God's action of giving Himself to us through His own body and blood. Both of these actions toward us are wrapped up in the greatest action of all: Christ's death and resurrection.

So, taking a cue from the common sign that reads "one way," go ahead and drive down your one-way street in prayer to God, loaded with thanksgiving, care, joy, need, complaint, praise, or any combination thereof, knowing that He is there listening and acting. And we live in the assurance that God's one-way street is aimed in our direction. He has promised to speak to us through His Word and His means of grace. Each day we can listen to Him comfort, encourage, and inspire us for the sake of His precious Son, Jesus Christ.

Following the one-way avenue to God, and listening to His one-way response to us, will keep us heading in the right direction.

Prayer

Dear Heavenly Father, we thank You for inviting us to talk to You anytime and about anything. Remove the worries that weigh us down and give us those gifts that will accomplish Your will among us. In Jesus' name. Amen.

For further reading ... Luke 11:1–13

Interstate 5 and U.S. Route 1

"Enter through the narrow gate. For wide is the gate and broad is the road that leads to destruction, and many enter through it. But small is the gate and narrow the road that leads to life, and only a few find it."
Matthew 7:13–14

There are two very different ways to travel from Los Angeles to the San Francisco area. They are Interstate 5 and U.S. Route 1.

Interstate 5 is relatively new, in every sense a modern freeway. It has two lanes of traffic traveling in both directions straight through the San Joaquin Valley. It was designed to move many vehicles quickly. Although the speed limit is 70, many vehicles pass your 70 as though you were standing still.

Some miles to the west is U.S. Route 1. It hugs the mountainous coastline of California, creating one exciting vista after another. It winds in and out, up and down for more than 100 miles. Each winter, some sections are closed because of washouts or bad weather. It is a two-lane road with "no passing" zones mile after mile, so travelers in a hurry are advised not to travel U.S. 1. The road was not designed for high speed or volume travel, but rather for breathtaking views and scenic enjoyment.

Perhaps Jesus could have used these two highways to contrast the way to salvation against the way to damnation. If life for us seems easy, unhindered, and full of agreeable fellow-travelers who whiz along with us, perhaps we need to examine on who's road we travel. Satan will never put up detour signs or caution lights as he hurries us on to eternal death. It is his desire that we travel his road unhindered.

But Jesus says, narrow is the road that leads to life. Besides the winding, curvy way, there are also sheer drop-offs that make each curve an adventure. For those who follow Christ along the route He carved out for us, life can be exciting, demanding, and at times even dangerous. And we must be careful to not be swayed by signs advertising Satan's major freeway only a couple miles away. Following Jesus is not easy and it certainly isn't popular.

But as we travel the sometimes lonely, winding road of life in Christ, we know where our journey will end. It will end at the narrow gate of heaven where Christ Himself will welcome us into our eternal home.

The narrow road is long and winding, but look Who is waiting for you at its end. Jesus has already traveled the road for you and has left His encouraging signs along the way: the Bible, His Sacraments, and our fellow travelers. Why be in a hurry when the scenery is so spectacular and our destination so assured?

Prayer

Dear Lord Jesus, we pray that You will accompany us on the way You have marked for us through life. Comfort us with Your presence and with the company of Your holy angels as we travel with You. Amen.

For further reading ... 2 Corinthians 11:16–33

Merging Traffic

**We live by faith, not by sight.
2 Corinthians 5:7**

You are doing 60 MPH in the middle lane. From the adjoining on-ramp appears a motorist also doing 60 MPH. Soon he will join you on the expressway in the lane at your right. Or will he? Perhaps he isn't paying attention and plans to move more to his left—directly into you! Assuming anything at 60 MPH only invites disaster. At this point your survival skills take over. You speed up, slow down, or change lanes to give him plenty of room.

Merging traffic doesn't happen only on expressways. We all know the feeling of being cramped or trapped in a mass of people. Many of us have experienced unexpected demands from our families when we don't need more responsibilities, the pushy co-worker who always seems to "be in our face," or the demanding boss who assumes we are property he or she can use and abuse at will. Life is full of merging traffic.

God also merged into our space. He left the glories of heaven to join us in the traffic jam of humanity. Not only did He join us, He absorbed all of our side-swipes and the ultimate head-on collision with sin at Calvary's cross.

St. Paul said, "We live by faith, not by sight." Living by faith in Christ, our Savior and Defender, means handing the wheel over to Him. Rather than allowing the traffic we see to upset us, we trust Christ as our Driver and Navigator. There's no need to fear when He is in the driver's seat. We know that as Christ endured the demolition derby of sin, He certainly will get us through our uncomfortable merges with the people in our lives and will deliver us safely to our eternal destination.

Prayer

Dear Lord Jesus, thank You for steering us in the right direction. Take charge of our lives so what we do and how we do it may be pleasing to our heavenly Father. In Your name we pray. Amen.

For further reading ... Philippians 2:1–18

Gapers Block

Each of you should look not only to your own interests, but also to the interests of others. Philippians 2:4

I've never heard the term "gapers block" used by anyone other than a traffic reporter named "Officer Vic" on WMAQ in Chicago in the late 1960s. He was referring to those maddening slow downs and complete stops on the expressways caused by motorists slowing or even stopping to gape at an accident.

While enduring the delay, many of us think, "How stupid!" Then, when we arrive at the accident scene, most of us also slow down to gape.

Gapers blocks are nothing more than humans caught up in their sinful natures. People are almost always fascinated by misfortune—as long as it is someone else's. That is why TV news never varies; each show could use the same pictures: fires, ambulances, police cars, and body bags. That is why checkout-counter tabloids are so popular. That is why church gossip is always about someone else doing something wrong. We have an insatiable appetite for disaster—as long as it's not our own.

Reading St. Paul's advice in context, we find in the preceding verse that our interest in others flows from a humble heart.

Paul wrote, "Do nothing out of selfish ambition or vain conceit, but in humility consider others better than yourselves" (Philippians 2:3).

These words tell us to have the attitude of Christ who humbled Himself for our sake. He willingly took our place in the burning building, in the wreck on the highway, and in the body bag. Christ is the only One who is perfect, yet He still gave His life to save wretched sinners.

Jesus caused His own gapers block as He healed the sick and honored social outcasts. Similarly, His followers also command attention when they selflessly reach out to the poor, sick, and afflicted. Instead of stopping to watch a tragedy unfold, Christians step in and offer help. They offer love and concern to their neighbors in need. Others notice these extraordinary acts of compassion. Jesus knew that God would be glorified through the actions of His followers, so He said, "That they may see your good deeds and praise your Father in heaven" (Matthew 5:16).

Instead of just being lookers, Christ's people are doers. Jesus said, "I tell you the truth, whatever you did for one of the least of these brothers of Mine, you did it for Me" (Matthew 25:40). Jesus came to earth for us. He sacrificed His life for us. Then He rose victorious from the grave. Now in response we love and help others with praise and thanksgiving for Jesus' sake. Let the world gape at the glory of Jesus that shines through you.

Prayer

Dear Lord Jesus, thank You for saving us from the disaster of sin. Help us now, on our road of life, to help where help is needed for Your sake. Let Your love shine through us as we care for others. We pray as You have taught us. Amen.

For further reading ... 1 Thessalonians 4:1–12

Land Barges

Then Jesus said to His disciples, "I tell you the truth, it is hard for a rich man to enter the kingdom of heaven." Matthew 19:23

Our campsite was near the entrance of the KOA where we were staying, providing us with a perfect view of a steady procession of campers as they registered for the night. We were amazed by the number of huge, 35-foot motor homes coming in. Attached to the rear of many of them were smaller vehicles, perhaps used to cruise the area after the motor homes were set up at their campsites or to drive to nearby grocery stories for provisions. They looked like land barges with little dinghies in tow.

When these rigs arrived at their assigned spot, they hooked up to water, electricity, and sewer. Then out came the array of "camping gear." Among these items might be the satellite dish, awning, gas grill, artificial green carpet, and string of camping lights. This was only on the outside. I can only imagine the comforts they enjoyed inside these portable palaces.

Perhaps if Jesus had been sitting at the same entrance and watching the same procession of opulence, He would have said,

"It is easier for a 35-foot Winnebago with a Saturn in tow to go through a car wash than for a rich person to enter heaven."

The entrance to God's Kingdom is through our Lord Jesus Christ. He alone is the gate. Even a life full of faithful church attendance, of generous offerings, and of congregational service cannot squeeze through the narrow gate of God's grace on its own merit. Heaven has no room for land barges full of good works. God's grace through Jesus Christ is the only thing we need. Our good works cannot earn us salvation because we are poor, miserable sinners.

This is not to say that good works aren't an important by-product of faith. God still calls us to do good works for our neighbors in response to His great love for us. He still calls us to spread the Good News of Jesus' life, death, and resurrection to everyone we meet. But we do all of these works for Jesus' sake, not our own.

Christ is the only entrance to heaven. As you enter God's heavenly campground, the only baggage you will see is what Christ Himself brought in—us. All other baggage will be unnecessary.

Prayer

Dear Father in heaven, as we continue down life's roads, keep us from collecting mementos of the good things we have done. Help us see these filthy rags laundered in the blood of Christ, our Savior. Accept these words, we pray, for the sake of Jesus, our Savior. Amen.

For further reading ... 2 Corinthians 12:1–10

39

Interstate 55

He makes grass grow for the cattle, and plants for man to cultivate—bringing forth food from the earth.
Psalm 104:14

Its formal name is Interstate 55 and its northernmost segment runs approximately 300 miles from Chicago to St. Louis through central Illinois. Years ago, it was part of U.S. Route 66, the Main Street of America.

Driving along this stretch of Interstate 55 is not demanding: no notable hills or curves or big cities. Staying awake is the problem. The scenery consists of cornfields, wheat fields, and bean fields—period! When discussing I-55, many motorists roll their eyes and heave a big sigh. To some, boring and I-55 have become synonymous.

However boring, this scenery provides a powerful testimony to the goodness of the Lord. With few exceptions, farmers plant their crops each year, apply fertilizer and herbicide, and the Lord takes care of the temperatures and the rainfall. The results are field after field of gigantic stalks of corn in dark green dress, lined up in perfect rows. Alternating with the corn is the green chenille texture of soybean fields and the golden velvet of ripened wheat. Again, man plants, God waters, and the earth brings forth another crop.

Unfortunately, some seasons do not produce a bumper crop. Every farm has seen its share of drought and flood. Even so, what affects one crop on I-55 affects them all. I have never seen a few prosperous-looking fields scattered among those that are ragged and barren. Summer thunderstorms rain equally on all the fields, just as the warm rays of the sun nourish all crops in their path. There is no distinction between the fields of the believing farmer and the unbelieving farmer. As Jesus points out in Matthew 5:45, "[God] causes His sun to rise on the evil and the good, and sends rain on the righteous and the unrighteous."

And the Lord doesn't stop with summer rain and sunshine. He showers His love on all humankind with the forgiveness earned for the world by Christ. Unfortunately, many hearts are closed to this gift. They are hard and unyielding, unwilling to acknowledge what God has done.

As God looks down from heaven, He sees barren, twisted, and misshapen fields of unbelievers. Therefore, God continually uses us to shower His love and mercy on those who are lost. He desires for the bountiful blessings He bestows on us to overflow onto our neighbors, friends, and even our enemies. Just as the corn and beans grow along I-55 season after season, God continues to plant faith in the hearts of people on earth.

Prayer

O Lord God, bless the efforts of those who work the land and provide food for your people. We also ask that You would give success to those who go forth and preach Your Word, sowing Your seeds as You have commanded. Nurture these seeds of faith in the hearts of all who do not yet believe. We ask this in Jesus' name. Amen.

For further reading ... Luke 10:1–20

Toll Roads

If he said "Sibboleth," because he could not pronounce the word correctly, they seized him and killed him at the fords of the Jordan. **Judges 12:6**

Does it seem that the verse above is from the middle of a story? You are right. And it is indeed a strange story.

After a war between the citizens of Gilead and those of Ephraim/Manasseh, Gilead came out on top. The victorious soldiers then captured one of the only crossing points over the Jordan River. As the defeated soldiers of Ephraim/Manasseh struggled to cross the river, the Gileadites waited for them. The test to see if they were from Gilead or from Ephraim/Manasseh was for each refugee to say the word "shibboleth." The people of Ephraim/Manasseh apparently could not pronounce the "sh" of shibboleth. So all who responded with "sibboleth" were killed on the spot.

That was quite a toll to pay to cross a river. Fortunately, we have to pay only a few coins at tollbooths today.

Although you may not know it, the world invokes a kind of toll nearly everyday. This toll, like the one extracted at the Jordan River, depends on what you do or do not say. You may pass without paying a toll if you *refrain* from speaking the name of Jesus Christ in a positive manner. If you happen to curse or use the name of Christ in vain, your reward will be free passage, maybe even a pat on the back. If, however, you speak about Jesus as your Savior and Lord, you pay a toll.

Many people do not wish to hear about Jesus Christ: His name, His work, or His effect on people. They are comfortable in their sin and do not want the Lord to shake up their lives. Today our society is building more and more of these toll roads in business, education, government, and certainly in entertainment. The name of Jesus becomes our "Shibboleth." If we say it the world's way, we may pass. If we say it Jesus' way, there may be a price to pay. We may be scorned, demoted, ridiculed, or ignored.

This comes as no surprise. Jesus tells us, "Blessed are you when people insult you, persecute you and falsely say all kinds of

evil against you because of Me"
(Matthew 5:11).

Pay attention to who is sitting at the window of society's tollbooth. You might recognize the same hand that reached out from the Garden of Eden. Although the devil continually makes traveling through life difficult and treacherous, be assured that God is always with you, knowing that Jesus will be coming soon to close the devil's toll road forever.

Prayer

Dear heavenly Father, increase our faith in Your promise to help and strengthen us as we make our way through life. Fill us with the riches of Your grace, so we may willingly pay the price of faithfulness to Your Word. Open our mouths to speak of You always. In the name of Jesus who gave His life and, even now, speaks up for us. Amen.

For further reading ... the book of Jude

Bugs on the Windshield

We saw the Nephilim there (the descendants of Anak come from the Nephilim). We seemed like grasshoppers in our own eyes, and we looked the same to them. Numbers 13:33

This passage is a turning point in the history of Israel. It is part of the report given by 10 of the spies Moses sent into Canaan to explore the land. Their entire report can be summarized in four words: "We can't do it!" Because of the Israelites' continued lack of faith, the Lord decided they would not enter the Promised Land. Forty years later, their descendants were allowed to enter.

To describe the Canaanites, these faithless spies compared them to the Nephilim, who were first named in Genesis 6:4. They supposedly were giants that lived on the earth before the Flood. They were warriors of great size and skill, representing evil in every respect. What better reference could be used to prove a point and scare the Israelites out of their wits?

Satan uses this same tactic when he tries to frighten believers away from God. He might sound something like this:

"You poor, deluded souls! You who claim to be God's sons and daughters. Look at you! If you are so valuable to God, where is the evidence? A lot of good your tithing does. You have to scrimp and save for every penny.

"And how about your standing in the community? Nobody knows you, and they don't want to know you. You abide by outdated commandments, while others ignore them and are a lot happier than you.

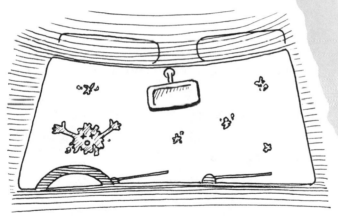

"How much has going to church benefited you? Look at the time you waste there. Weekends are too short to spend time with a bunch of hypocrites being bored with stuff you've heard and done a thousand times."

Satan would have us believe that we are like bugs squashed on the windshield of time. He tells us that time is moving fast, and instead of keeping up, we're wasting it with God.

You may have noticed that quietly left out of Satan's harangue is any reference to Jesus Christ. This is because it was Jesus who once and for all defeated Satan at Calvary, where He met him head-on. And note that this collision was already reported in Genesis, chapter 3.

Satan is the real bug on the windshield. Jesus flattened him thousands of years ago. Unfortunately, Satan's lips still move—but with Christ in control, it's only talk.

Prayer

Dear Jesus, we thank and praise You for redeeming us from sin and darkness. Continue to defend us from Satan's daily temptation to make us feel small. Empower us to live each day in the confidence of Your victory over Satan. Amen.

For further reading ... Matthew 4:1–11

Strange Noises

"Come, let us go down and confuse their language so they will not understand each other." Genesis 11:7

When you buy a new car, it looks new, it smells new, and it even sounds new. Each component seems to work perfectly with the next, creating a quiet hum of automotive contentment.

As time goes on, however, you may begin to notice deviations: a clunk instead of a swish; a squeak instead of silence; a rumble where the quiet hum once existed. Your car is talking to you. Its message? "I need help!"

The occupants of the Shinar Valley also spoke a language of dissension and turmoil, much like the grumbling of a worn-out car. Their message? "God, we will do things our way. We will not disperse and fill the earth as You said. Instead we will build a city and a tower and we will become famous for it."

Our heavenly Father heard and saw this deviation from His will. He heard their defiance and witnessed their construction of a tower that was supposed to reach to heaven. God answered their defiance and egotism by confusing their language. They suddenly could not understand one another. They couldn't continue building the tower because they couldn't communicate. The people of the Shinar Valley did not make a name for themselves because of their great achievement. They made a name for themselves because of their great disorder—"Babel," which means "confused."

God still hears strange noises from us. He hears the irritating grinding of the friction between us and others; the ear-splitting squeal of relationships that have run out of oil; the recurring thump, thump of those who stumble along trying to serve both the true God and other gods. But the Lord has quieted all of these noises through the work of His Son. Jesus covers them all with the blood of His sacrifice.

Unfortunately, the clamor of sin still penetrates our hearing and disturbs us on our journey. We live in a confused world where many search in vain for satisfaction and esteem apart from God. We daily struggle with our own sinful nature. We know that our only hope of salvation rests in God's grace and forgiveness for the sake of Jesus Christ.

As we quietly proclaim the Good News of God's grace, the Holy Spirit continues to work faith in the hearts of those who are confused. Perhaps through us, they might finally hear the Good News God is proclaiming.

Prayer

Dear Lord, help us to shut out the confusing noises of the world. Open our ears so we may hear You through Your Word. Open our mouths so we may tell of the wonders of Your grace by the power of the Holy Spirit. Open the hearts of those who hear Your Word that they too may come to faith and proclaim Your love in Christ, in whose name we pray. Amen.

For further reading ... Acts 2:1–41

That Little Yellow Line

Yet as surely as the LORD lives and as you live, there is only a step between me and death.
1 Samuel 20:3

Saul was trying his best to kill David. He had tried to stab him with his spear several times and had sent his servants and officials to capture him on several other occasions. Saul was jealous of David's success and was willing to do anything to keep David from becoming the next King of Israel. That is why David said, "There is only a step between me and death." He was constantly on the run from Saul.

The only reason David survived at all was because of the Lord's protection. God had a plan for David and there was nothing Saul could do to interfere with that plan. The Lord was the step between David and death.

As we continue our journeys, we realize that we too are only a step away from death. On the highway, only a little yellow line separates us from 10 tons of onrushing steel. How often have we unknowingly been passed by drivers who were half-asleep, under the influence of alcohol, or paying more attention to their passenger, radio, or cell phone than their driving?

On life's journeys, the little yellow line takes the form of a parent's advice, a friend's intervention, a doctor's diagnosis, or a caution from God's Word. In all of these instances, God uses the little yellow line to keep us on the path to eternal life He has marked out for us.

This line, however, is not yellow. It's red. It is the line drawn on Calvary with the blood of Christ. His precious blood separates us from a head-on collision with Satan and his load of accusations and guilt that would certainly crush us. If it were not for God's costly barrier of Christ's death, we would all be just a step away from eternal death.

As the little yellow line on the highway zips by mile after mile, be reminded that God's red line of love separates us from eternal death. Share this good news with your fellow travelers.

Prayer

Our Father, we thank You for protecting us each day from dangers both at home and on the road. We also thank You for the protection of Your holy angels as they accompany us in the way we should go. In Jesus' name we pray. Amen.

For further reading ... 1 Samuel 20:1–42

Washboard Avenue

Every valley shall be raised up, every mountain and hill be made low; the rough ground shall become level, the rugged places a plain. Isaiah 40:4

The people of Isaiah's day would have recognized the actions of this passage as a customary way to welcome visiting kings and other high officials. It was unthinkable to subject an important visitor to steep grades, rough roads, and treacherous impasses.

When Isaiah says in verse 3 that this is to be a highway for the Lord, the preparations for His arrival become even more important. The King of Kings is on His way. Be ready!

We have heard these words many times, especially during Advent. During this season, Messianic prophecies are read and heard quite frequently. "Yes, yes," we yawn, "Christmas is coming and there is a lot to get done." Then many of us return to our frantic preparations, ignoring what God is really saying through the words of Isaiah.

Perhaps some of you have experienced stretches of highway that are heavily traveled by 18-wheelers. The pavement is broken. Many times the expansion joints have been pounded

into gigantic bumps that rattle the suspension of even the most plush automobiles. I imagine this bone-jarring ride is what our Lord often experiences as He takes residence in our hearts.

Our lives are so frantic that all Jesus finds is the constant vibration of our earthly desires, frenetic dashes from one self-serving goal to another—all punctuated by the sounds of a world gone mad. The Holy Spirit quiets this cacophony and restores order as He prepares our hearts for the Lord Jesus. Ever since the Holy Spirit entered our hearts at Baptism, He has been preparing a quiet dwelling within us for our Savior.

Worldly cares continue to pound on us like 18-wheelers. Sleek convertibles with loads of lust traverse our hearts in a never-ending stream. Especially at Christmas, we notice Santa's sleigh, grossly overweight, plowing up our lives with the trappings of materialism and greed that have sadly become synonymous with this holy holiday.

Before getting carried away by sinful desire, listen to the real message of Isaiah: Cut down on the traffic! Repair the roads of your minds and hearts. Outlaw the overweight vehicles of greed. Pay attention as the Holy Spirit prepares your heart to receive Jesus—not just at Christmastime, but at all times. Jesus is coming for sure, but we don't know when. We don't know how many repair days we have left. Be ready.

Prayer

O, dearest Jesus, holy child,
Prepare a bed, soft, undefiled;
A holy shrine, within my heart,
That you and I need never part. Amen.

For further reading ... Joel 2:12–17

The Card Reader

LORD, You have searched me and You know me. You know when I sit and when I rise; You perceive my thoughts from afar. Psalm 139:1-2

One of the marvels of the computer age is the credit card reader at the gas pump. It has become a standard method of paying for gas. At some gas stations, you can wave a little gizmo on your key chain in front of the flying red horse. He immediately lights up and the pump turns on. You fill up the tank and receive a receipt with everything printed about you—except, perhaps, your mother's maiden name.

All of this technology bothers some people. They may appreciate the speed and convenience of the equipment, but they are disturbed that someone somewhere has access to their financial and personal information.

Perhaps the words from today's Scripture reading are just as disconcerting. The Lord knows everything about us. He has searched every person thoroughly. He alone knows what each of us looks like on the inside.

That level of intimacy makes some squirm. An unbeliever might become disturbed at the news of a God who is forever poking into his or her affairs. This is evidence of living outside God's Kingdom—evidence of the effects of God's Law upon their hearts.

God has told us what is right and wrong through His Word and by writing His Law on our hearts. We know we are wretched and miserable sinners. When our heavenly Father looks at us in His glorious perfection, we can't help but be ashamed. We squirm and recoil from the white light scrutiny of a righteous God.

Thankfully, God no longer sees our sins when He looks at us. Instead, He sees the blood Jesus shed for us on the cross. Jesus suffered the Lord's just wrath in our place so we can be reconciled to God. We have become God's children through the waters of Baptism and are daily strengthened in the faith.

Instead of being uncomfortable with God's knowledge of our heart, take comfort in His unconditional love and mercy.

Say, "Lord, You know me better than I know myself. You know what I really need and what I don't. Your guidance and protection are with me always. You know my thoughts and You always hear my prayers. All my wretched sins have been forgiven in Your boundless grace."

When calling on God, we don't need a card or a card reader. He is there already and has filled our tank—and charged it all to Jesus.

Prayer

Dear Lord God, we joyfully acknowledge Your presence in our lives. We delight in Your knowing our comings and goings; our ups and downs; our delights and dismays. We pray that as our lives unfold, we may never lose sight of Your guiding hand, pointing us in the way of Christ. According to Your will, bring others to this same joyful knowledge. We pray as did Jesus, our Savior. Amen.

For further reading ... John 21:15–25

The Good Hands People

> "He will call upon Me and I will answer him; I will be with him in trouble, I will deliver him and honor him. With long life will I satisfy him and show him My salvation." Psalm 91:15–16

Talk to any teenager who has just become the owner of a car and you will hear a moan when the subject of insurance comes up. Gas and minor upkeep expenses are tolerable, but insurance premiums are unbearable.

It is much the same for all car owners. Insurance is a major expenditure. What's worse is that the rates seem to be increasing. Insurance companies have a fail-safe system: if their expenses go up, premiums go up.

What if God treated us the same way insurance companies do? What if He promised to take care of us as long as we kept up with our church contributions? Would God raise our rates if we presented too many claims for help? Twice each year we might receive a bill noting whether we would receive a discount for good behavior.

As foolish as this sounds, there are many Christians who view God as a kind of divine insurance broker. They feel that the number of blessings they receive is directly proportional to the amount they contribute to church, to how well they obey God's laws, and to how often they go to church. When they do all of these good works, they expect God to take care of them and respond instantly in an emergency.

Some people have not yet realized that God's plan of salvation isn't a business. It's a gift. His protection and help are free. He even dispatches angels to guard us on our way. And, thanks to Jesus, He doesn't require premium payments. He has thrown away our driving records. We receive no semi-annual bill and there is never a rate increase.

Forgiveness in our earthly lives and the salvation of our eternal destiny have been paid for. Jesus' hands bear the imprint of the one and only premium payment. In joyful response, we worship, feast at the Lord's Table, obey His laws, and tell others of this wonderful news. We know we can't do anything to earn God's gifts of love and forgiveness. All we can do is praise and thank Him with the lives He bought for us with His Son's precious blood.

We are truly and eternally insured by one who is far greater than the Good Hands People, the one and only true God—Father, Son, and Holy Spirit.

Prayer

O blessed Trinity; Father, Son, and Spirit, we praise You for Your divine plan to insure our life with You forever. We thank You for our lives here on earth and for the payment made for our sins. We thank You for the beginning You made in our hearts through Baptism. And we thank and praise You for Your unconditional love earned us by the blood of Christ, in whose name we pray. Amen.

For further reading ... John 20:19–31

A Day in the Life of a Cow

But now, this is what the LORD says—He who created you, O Jacob, He who formed you, O Israel: "Fear not, for I have redeemed you; I have summoned you by name; you are Mine." Isaiah 43:1

While driving on a rural highway, have you ever wondered about the life of a cow? Have you ever wondered about the lifestyle of the thousands of cattle that dot the hillsides in every corner of our land? Some roam free, as in Colorado, rarely seeing humans. Some are crammed together in smelly pens, called feed lots, or spend their whole lives in barns. Still others, specifically dairy cows, munch the green grass of a Midwest pasture.

It seems that a cow's life revolves around the daily search for something to eat. They sleep. They eat. They walk. They eat.

They stand. They eat, and so on. This continues until they die. Cows are living commodities that come and go. Their value is completely dependent on how they are consumed—either as milk or as hamburger.

In Satan's eyes, human beings are just like cattle. Whether we live in congested cities, sprawling suburbs, or in tiny towns, Satan sees us as nothing more than stupid animals to rustle away from God. Satan knows that God loves His creation. He knows that God especially loves human beings who were created in His own image. Therefore, Satan tries to seduce us away from saving faith and grace in a spiteful effort to hurt God. Satan's pastures and feed lots are fenced by sin and obsession. He convinces people to be content with meager pleasures, temporary playthings, and full stomachs.

But over this sad scene comes the majestic voice of God, "I created all of you; I redeemed you for the sake of My Son, Jesus Christ. His death on the cross saved you from sin, death, and the power of the devil. I know each of you by name, the name that I called you at your Baptism. You are Mine."

We are not commodities to be bought, sold, and slaughtered. We are the eternal sons and daughters of God, the Creator and Ruler of all—even the pseudo cattle baron, Satan.

All that remains to confirm our true identity is the last roundup, yet to come. And that is coming soon.

Yee Haa!

Prayer

O heavenly Father, we thank You for creating us, choosing us, buying us back, and now feeding us with Your true Word and giving us to drink of the heavenly waters of life. Preserve us, O Father, from the wily assaults of Satan who would convince us that we are merely cattle. Assure us that we are Your special children. We pray in the name of Jesus, our sacrificial Lamb. Amen.

For further reading ... Job 1:1–22

Botts' Dots

Your word is a lamp to my feet and a light for my path. Psalm 119:105

You drive over them and beside them. When you can't see them, you may become apprehensive. Those reflective bumps in the pavement that mark lanes on highways can be reassuring. In California they are called Botts' Dots. In northern states, where raised bumps might be destroyed by snowplows, the reflective strips are called Life-Lites.

The ancestor of Botts' Dots was invented in England during WWII. Blackouts prohibited streetlights, so an ingenious citizen laid out reflective metal strips to guide emergency vehicles.

In California, an engineer named Botts installed the first raised, ceramic bumps on the Golden Gate Bridge in 1963 to avoid the hassle of repainting traffic lines.

In 1977, Ohio Governor James Rhodes led the installation of snowplow-proof, recessed, reflective strips on Ohio's major highways. Now most states have installed them, resulting in much safer and less frightening night travel.

Perhaps the human author of Psalm 119 might have rephrased verse 105 had he traveled on Judean roads that were marked with Botts' Dots and Life-Lites. He might then have written, "Your words are Botts' Dots to my feet and Life-Lites to mark my path."

One advantage of Botts' Dots is that you can feel them. If you accidentally cross into an adjoining lane, they cause a vibration in your car. This is a lot like God's Law. His Law causes an unnerving vibration in our hearts and minds when we cross into the dangerous lane of sin. The psalmist writes, "By [the commands of the Lord] is Your servant warned" (Psalm 19:11). How foolish then for us to stay in the wrong lane after being alerted by God's Law in our hearts and minds.

Life-Lites are more difficult to feel. Even so, they guide us when snow and ice obstruct our view. Life-Lites can survive the impact of snowplows and the decay caused by road salt. God's Word is as obvious and constant as the durable Life-Lites.

His reassuring words of comfort, heard and seen through the life and death of Jesus Christ, are there to remind you of His constant love. Even when the snowstorms of life threaten to cover your way, Christ is there with the light of His love to lead you to safety. No wonder He says, "I am the Light of the world" (John 8:12). His glorious light leads the way.

Botts' Dots and Life-Lites will continue to perform their life-saving duty on the highways and interstates, just as God's Word will continue to guide us and shine His everlasting light in our lives.

Prayer

Dear Lord Jesus, we thank You for the light of Your divine presence in our lives. We thank You for guiding us in Your Word through the darkness of the world and for warning us through Your Word when we are in spiritual danger. Continue to light our paths as You lead us to heaven. In Your holy name we pray. Amen.

For further reading ... Psalm 119:33–40

The Lane Changers

> "No one can serve two masters. Either he will hate the one and love the other, or he will be devoted to the one and despise the other. You cannot serve both God and Money."
> Matthew 6:24

You have seen them. You might even be one of them. Lane changers! They dart in and out of traffic, never content to adopt the general pace. If a car-sized gap appears to the right or left, they are in it. But only for a moment. When the next opening appears, they quickly pop in, staying there just until they can change lanes again. All this in an effort to gain a few extra minutes, with little regard for the safety of their fellow motorists.

Some people live like lane changers in their daily life. Whatever is new or popular or "in," whatever will give them a slight advantage, is what they want to have or where they want to be. Allegiance to a former belief or practice seems passé. Vows and promises become as permanent as smoke on a windy day.

Lane changers strike in personal relationships as well. Many times they rush into marriage, caught up in their feelings of lust and excitement. However, after a few months or years, the lane changer becomes bored. The relationship doesn't seem as fun and exciting as it did at the outset. And they begin looking for a new lane.

Many congregations feel they need to change lanes to effectively reach out to today's diverse and evolving society. While there is definitely a need to reach out to people in our changing world, changing the church isn't something to be taken lightly. The danger is that while the transformed church appeals to the ideals and values of society, it risks remaining faithful to God and His teachings in the Bible.

Thankfully, Jesus wasn't a lane changer. He was given a very difficult task, and He followed the plan perfectly. He veered neither to the right nor to the left, although He had plenty of opportunity. He didn't follow the crowd, and He didn't cut people off for His own advancement. Instead, Jesus assumed the terrible driving record of all of lane changers, taking our sinful infractions to the cross. The perfect completion of His Father's plan has paid the price in full. Because of Christ's unconditional commitment to us, we will one day live with Him in heaven.

Jesus stayed focused and truly followed His heavenly Father. And now God urges you and me to quit changing lanes, to finally realize that He is our loving and wise Leader, our sure route. Jesus urges us to stay in the lane that God has chosen for us. Following Him, we know where we are going and how to get there.

Would it be too simple to say that staying in the same lane lets us enjoy the ride and the view?

Prayer

Dear Lord Jesus, forgive us for the many times we have left the narrow path You paved. Forgive our impatience with others and with You. Give us the spiritual maturity to journey through life with joy and dedication only to You. Through You we pray. Amen.

For further reading ... Matthew 6:19–34

Wine is a mocker and beer a brawler; whoever is led astray by them is not wise. Proverbs 20:1

We are so used to hearing "Don't drink and drive!" that we have almost tuned out its message. Alcohol has such a grasp on society that although people know better, some still continue to drink and drive.

Perhaps you can recall that eerie feeling of not quite being in control after just a few drinks. The alertness required when driving is dulled with just a drink or two.

But driving under the influence is just the beginning of the problem. The writer of Proverbs delves even further into the dangers. He wrote, "Wine is a mocker." It makes fun of us, turning us into caricatures. He continues, "Beer [is] a brawler." It lowers our safeguards. We consider ourselves invincible. We don't feel any pain, and sometimes we even verbally or emotionally assault those we care about.

Such is the power of sin. It is just as intoxicating, just as damaging, and much more dangerous than alcohol. We don't have to eat or drink anything to be affected. Sin is an inherited part of our human nature. As we drive through life under sin's influence, we careen from curb to curb, propelled by a selfish desire to enjoy more—even at the expense of others. Satan is always the back-seat driver, encouraging us to have another. He doesn't care if we end our lives in crumpled heaps of eternal death.

What is God doing while we are spinning out of control? He is patiently offering us the one, sure cure for spiritual drunkenness: the innocent blood of His own Son. When Jesus gave His life for ours, He conquered the intoxicating power of sin. Although we still face temptations, because of Jesus' victory over sin and through the power of the Holy Spirit, we have the means to resist sin and remain faithful to God. Jesus infuses us with His own life through the waters of Baptism and through His body and blood in Holy Communion. So as a forgiven and redeemed child of God, know that you drive under His gracious and loving influence.

Prayer

O Lord Jesus, please forgive us when we become intoxicated by sin. Fill us with Your grace that we may joyfully live the life You have given us. Help us to gladly witness Your loving faithfulness to others. In Your name we pray. Amen.

For further reading ... Proverbs 23:30–35

Interstate 70

When times are good, be happy; but when times are bad, consider: God has made the one as well as the other. Therefore, a man cannot discover anything about his future. Ecclesiastes 7:14

The author of Ecclesiastes evidently was one of us. He admitted that there are some times in life that are absolutely enjoyable, but there are also bad times. In particular, his conclusion arouses our interest.

To illustrate this, let's use Interstate 70 between Maryland and central Utah. Between these two points is a great amount of contrasting scenery and travel conditions: rolling hills, green forests, and interesting towns; big city traffic where the roads seem to be in a perpetual state of construction; the plains with their subtle beauty; the striking beauty of the Rocky Mountains; and finally, a 100-mile stretch where there are no services of any kind. With this in mind, Interstate 70 completes its parallel to life: some ups, some downs, good spots, some bad.

This is where the writer of Ecclesiastes makes his point. God is the author of hill and valley, loneliness and traffic, new pavement and cracked, curves and straightaways. We must remember, however, that God does not construct the obstacles in life. They are the result of our sinful world and our human weakness.

God knows that we will face trials and temptations every day of our earthly journey. That's why He sent His Son. Through Jesus' victory, God gives us the power and strength to endure the unbearable.

Though He does not construct the obstacles of life, God does allow these challenges to confront us. St. Paul often listed the good things along with the bad as he traveled his version of I-70. In particular we remember his "thorn in the flesh," as he describes it: "a messenger of Satan to torment me" (2 Corinthians 12:7). His conclusion about that "thorn" is Paul's answer to the point made in Ecclesiastes.

TOO HIGH PASS
EL. 11,000 FT.

"Therefore, a man cannot discover anything about his future," says Ecclesiastes. For Paul and for us, his answer to the future is what God told him: "My grace is sufficient for you, for My power is made perfect in weakness" (2 Corinthians 12:9).

We know there is an I-70 before us with ups and downs, goods and bads. Also before us is a Savior who walked His I-70 alone, and perfectly, for all of us. Therefore when the road is easy and the view is great, thank the Lord for His goodness and blessings. When the grade is steep, the traffic unbearable, and the weather foul, trust the Lord. For He has been this way before. He has left His markers for you to see and in Him you can take comfort.

Prayer

Dear Lord and Savior, sometimes we are fearful of the road ahead. Please take our hands and lead us through the valleys of shadow and towns of terror. Assure us of Your presence each day, as we see You in the pages of Scripture loving, leading, dying, and rising for us. In You we pray. Amen.

For further reading ... Psalm 141

The Tailgater

Be self-controlled and alert. Your enemy the devil prowls around like a roaring lion looking for someone to devour. 1 Peter 5:18

It takes only a glance in the rearview mirror to spot him. He is so close you can't even see his headlights. If you suddenly stop, he will run right into your trunk—or maybe worse. You have been beset by a tailgater!

What has motivated this person to not just endanger himself, but you and others as well? Perhaps he wants you to drive faster or to get out of his way so he can drive faster. Perhaps he just enjoys irritating people. Whatever the reason, tailgaters are a menace.

In your spiritual walk through life, do you ever get the feeling that you are being tailgated? As you look backward, are you aware of one who dogs your steps, never letting you forget that he is there? The tailgater is Satan, and we know exactly why he is there.

St. Peter uses the word "devour." Satan would love to swallow us whole with his waves of accusations, his streams of guilt, and his deluge of temptations. No matter where we are in life, Satan is there, leering at us in the rearview mirror.

Peter's advice to his fellow believers is to be self-controlled and alert, but to remember that trying to outrun or out-maneuver Satan is futile. Human resources are powerless against the devil. St. Paul says in Ephesians 6:12, "Our struggle is not against flesh and blood, but against the rulers, against the authorities, against the powers of this dark world and against the spiritual forces of evil in the heavenly realms." Without the power and grace of God, we have as much chance of outsmarting Satan as a Yugo has of outrunning a Porsche.

By the power of the Holy Spirit, being self-controlled and alert is our only defense against Satan. We rely on Jesus Christ who already has taken the air out of his tires and emptied his tank. Through Jesus, Satan has already been arrested. Jesus stands between us and Satan, now and forever. Satan cannot harm anyone who is in Christ.

Christ expects us to continue living life following His lead. Even so, Paul tells us to keep our eyes on all mirrors and to the front because we don't know where Satan will appear next.

Despite how intimidating and ferocious Satan may appear, the Holy Spirit equips us to guard against all temptations. As God's children, we take comfort and confidence in Christ's victory over Satan. Remember that all you can see are the devil's headlights—he is running out of gas!

Prayer

Dear Lord Jesus, thank You for defeating Satan. Keep us aware of this glorious truth, especially as he tries to pull us away from You. Send Your Holy Spirit to keep us attached to You and Your promises. Send Your angels to protect us from all danger as we continue on the road of life. As you have commanded, so we pray. Amen.

For further reading ... Ephesians 6:10–20

God's Techs

For He will command His angels concerning you to guard you in all your ways; they will lift you up in their hands, so that you will not strike your foot against a stone. Psalm 91:11–12

Each reader of Psalm 91:11–12, no doubt has his or her own image of how God's angels perform this most welcome duty. From the old picture of the angel guarding two children as they cross a stream to the recent deluge of guardian angel pins, everyone sees this blessing in his or her own way.

"In all your ways ..." as the psalmist puts it, certainly includes our modern ways of travel. While "not striking our foot against a stone" fits the foot traveler of

Bible times, could this translate to expressway motorists, airline passengers, and cruise ship patrons as well?

When was the last time you checked all 20 lug nuts on your car's wheels or inspected each belt on the engine? How long has it been since you personally examined every inch of wiring for worn insulation or loose connections? Most of us never check these things, yet our automobiles usually remain quite reliable. And then there are the thousands of other cars and trucks on the road, and for the most part they too seem to operate reasonably well.

Perhaps this can point to God keeping His promise to protect us "in all our ways" through the ministry of His holy angels. Many Christians have stories of how they miraculously escaped with little or no harm from a would-be highway disaster. Often they have no explanation for their remarkable reprieve other than the intervention of God's holy angels. If God has provided us with angels who have mastered car upkeep and traffic control and electronic monitoring, wouldn't He also give personal attention to our spiritual safekeeping?

Of course He would. God is the supreme Technician who correctly diagnosed our sinful and hopeless human condition. He sent His Son Jesus as the only One who could repair our broken down lives. He suffered and died to save us from the awful wreckage of sin. He forgave us and promised us the glory of eternal life in heaven through His gracious and unconditional love. Unlike an earthly mechanic, Jesus both performed and paid for our spiritual repairs. And we can't even fathom the cost. Only God could—and did.

God's garage certainly has provided us with technicians to assist us in our journey here and will accompany us to our life in heaven.

Prayer

Dear heavenly Father, we thank You for the constant care You provide through Your holy angels. Through Your Word, guide us in Your ways. Restore us through Your Holy Meal. Strengthen our character and mind by the power of the Holy Spirit to keep us in Your holy ways. In Jesus' name. Amen.

For further reading ... Acts 12:1–19

Potholes

The arrogant dig pitfalls for me, contrary to Your law. Psalm 119:85

No better conspiracy can be found than the sudden appearance of potholes. These yawning holes appear suddenly on roads where smooth pavement once existed. As the sun warms the ice in the cracks, it takes just one car wheel to dislodge a chunk of pavement. Before long, that small chunk of loose pavement becomes a big hole.

The road department frantically tries to keep ahead of the outbreak. Sometimes it has to repair the same stretch of road twice in one day. On many occasions, it ends up patching the patches. Then there's the damage done to car suspensions, tires, and motorists' bank accounts.

In Psalm 119:85, the psalmist refers to pitfalls dug by "the arrogant." He may as well have called them potholes. Only these potholes are not the result of freezing and thawing and heavy traffic. They are the result of sinful mouths that love to dig craters in other people's reputations.

Sad to say this dreadful outbreak is not just the handiwork of unbelievers. God's children are especially vulnerable to this sin and often create potholes of arrogance. The height of arrogance is reached when we dig up other people's faults while ignoring our own. Jesus asked, "Why do you look at the speck of sawdust in your brother's eye and pay no attention to the plank in your own eye?" (Luke 6:41).

Our lives are full of potholes we have dug ourselves, and there is no way we can attempt to repair the damage on our own. Only Jesus can fix the potholes in our lives with the innocent blood He shed for us on the cross. Through daily study in the Word and through the means of God's grace, the Holy Spirit fills and patches these holes in our character. Empowered by the Spirit, we can reach out to our neighbors with the Good News of God's grace and forgiveness.

Prayer

O, gracious Savior, thank You for forgiving us for our arrogance. Help us to recognize slander and avoid it. Fill our mouths with Your praise and encouragement for others, especially when they are not present. In Your name we pray. Amen.

For further reading ... James 3:1–12

A Fading Signal

I am a stranger on earth; do not hide Your commands from me. Psalm 119:19

How comforting, when driving on a lonely stretch of road, to have the company of the radio. In addition to the sound it makes, there is always the curiosity about local news. We may not know the advertisers or the people named, but it is fascinating to listen to information about the passing towns and their goings-on.

That's why the inevitable crack and buzz that occur as we drive out of range of the radio signal is frustrating. Just as we are getting interested in the price of corn futures or pork bellies, the sound fades. Then, as we finally head down a long hill, the station is gone.

The author of Psalm 119 expresses a similar concern about God's Word in his life. He realized He was just a stranger on earth. Therefore, the psalmist was concerned about keeping in touch with God's commands as he traveled.

Perhaps, at one time in our lives, the signal of God's presence came in loud and clear. We listened each day to His Word read and explained. Then, as we traveled farther from the presence of God, the signal began to fade. Perhaps we didn't even notice because our attention was fixed on the passing scenery. Maybe our trip continued so far from His presence that the comforting voice of God turned into static.

Be assured that God does not move. We are the ones who journey away from Him. God constantly broadcasts His message of love, forgiveness, and salvation through His Word and Sacraments. God's transmitter is in the shape of a cross, and the signal is steady and strong. His message can reach us wherever you are, as long as you aren't tuning Him out. It is by this constant broadcasting of God's grace that lost travelers are brought back to the circle of God's love.

Prayer

O merciful Father in heaven, forgive us for tuning You out. Lead us to worship and to Your Word, so we may not stray from Your ways. Encourage us with the knowledge that Jesus is our fellow traveler and the Holy Spirit is our faithful Guide. In the name of our Savior we pray. Amen.

For further reading ... Isaiah 55:1–13

How's Your Mileage?

"From everyone who has been given much, much will be demanded; and from the one who has been entrusted with much, much more will be asked." Luke 12:48

Do you remember the gas shortages of the early '70s? Motorists eagerly searched for the green flag at gas stations indicating that gas could be purchased. Some areas had an "odd-even days" system: You could buy gas when the last digit of your license plate matched the odd or even number of the date. Such measures were taken to spread around the limited supply of gasoline.

For the first time, drivers were forced to become aware of economic gas mileage. Small, fuel-efficient cars were in demand, while the huge, chrome-encrusted gas-guzzlers were found on the used-car lot .

God is similarly concerned with our mileage. He fills us each day with overflowing mercy and grace as He forgives our sins for Jesus' sake. God desires for us to respond to His unconditional gifts of grace and forgiveness. He has given us immeasurable blessings and enables each of us to "travel" in His name for as many miles as He wills.

We gladly accept God's free grace, but to what extent do we respond? Considering the forgiveness we have received, do we forgive others? With all of the talents and abilities each of us have received, are we using them for God's glory?

If a car's mileage decreases, a tune-up is in order. So it is with God's children. Do we feed our faith with the words and promises of God? Do we find it difficult to express our faith in word or deed? Is the spark of our love and devotion weak and our exhaust plugged? If so, we can ask the Holy Spirit to restore us with Christ-motivated love. With all that Jesus spent on us—even His very life, we can now emerge into life energized by His resurrection and powered for eternity. Pray that the Holy Spirit will give you more faith miles to the gallon.

Prayer

Dear Lord Jesus, You showered Your immeasurable love on us as You paid for all of our sins on Calvary's cross. We pray that as Your Spirit strengthens our faith, we may live our lives in thanksgiving to You. Give us opportunities to forgive, help, comfort, and encourage those who need Your love. We thank You for giving us so much; help us now to return it to You through others. For You live and reign with the Father and the Holy Spirit, One God, now and forever. Amen.

For further reading ... James 4:14–26

Salt on the Road

"You are the salt of the earth." Matthew 5:13

For thousands of years, because there was no refrigeration, salt was used as a preservative to keep meat and fish from spoiling. Jesus used the metaphor in today's Bible passage to teach about living the life of a disciple—His disciple—as salt in a world rotting from sin.

Today we have refrigeration and countless chemicals that help preserve food. Yet to hear Jesus say, "You are the potassium sorbate of the earth," or "the Kenmore of the earth," just doesn't have the same ring. Perhaps, the salt metaphor could also be applied in a different context.

This analogy could remind us of what happens when winter roads become slippery with ice and snow. The highway department spreads sodium chloride. The salt mixes with the snow and ice, lowers its freezing temperature, and turns it into water again. Car and truck tires are then less likely to slip and spin and more likely to grip the pavement for traction and for stopping.

Christ uses His disciples in a world that is rapidly sliding away from God. Sinful humans lose control on the slick ice of self-fulfillment, self-importance, and self-worth. Some people don't even realize they are in need of forgiveness. Some don't understand how much they need God's love and redemption.

The message of Christ's love dissolves the treachery of this world and brings the hearer back to the basics: Humans are sinful; we all deserve eternal death. And this message of Good News also gives a world of despair some-

thing to stick to: God loved us so much that He sent His only Son to take our sins to the cross. We are forgiven and free to love others in Christ and spread the salt—the wonderful news of salvation.

Our lives of discipleship and verbal witness can be the very salt of which Jesus spoke. The world needs to see people who do not slip and slide at every turn in the road. They need to see that Christ enables us to make our way safely through any blizzard Satan blows our way.

You are the salt of the earth, just as Jesus said. Continue to spread His saving salt by the power of the Holy Spirit to all those whose hearts are cold and icy.

Prayer

Thank You, O Lord, for using us as the salt of the earth, testifying to Your presence in the world. Make us effective in our witness of both Law and Gospel. Enable us to keep Your message strong and clear through our words and actions. Fill us with your Holy Spirit as we strive to bring glory to You. In Jesus' name. Amen.

For further reading ... 1 Peter 4:1–11

Roadkill

As for you, you were dead in your transgressions and sins. Ephesians 2:1

This is a travel-related topic for those with strong stomachs: The topic? Dead animals on the highway. Roadkill is certainly a disgusting sight.

I bring this up because the gruesome sight of roadkill reminds me of our own death in sin, just as St. Paul said in Ephesians 2:1, "You were dead in your transgressions and sins." Although you may have heard this verse many times, have you even really thought about the reality of what Paul was saying?

In the beginning, God created humans in His own image. Adam and Eve were completely perfect and without sin. However, when they ate the forbidden fruit, their perfection was taken away by the deadly grip of sin. They foolishly traded in their gracious gift of life for the grotesque ugliness of sin and death. Roadkill—squashed on the side of the road by Satan.

It was then that God said He would not merely scoop us up and dispose of us. He determined to preserve us. The fact that we have been made spiritually alive is completely God's miracle. He told Satan that He would send someone to destroy him and restore us to life once again. God sent His

Son, Jesus, to earth to take the punishment we deserve onto Himself. Ephesians 2:4–5 says, "But because of His great love for us, God, who is rich in mercy, made us alive with Christ even when we were dead in transgressions—it is by grace you have been saved."

None of us can even remotely take credit for our rebirth into Christ's death and resurrection. A pile of broken bones and rotting flesh cannot say, "And then I decided to accept Christ and to live for Him." We were roadkill—dead, decaying, and disgusting.

But God graciously restored us by sacrificing Jesus for our sins. And how did God do this? 2 Corinthians says, "God made Him who had no sin, to be sin for us, so that in Him we might become the righteousness of God" (2 Corinthians 5:21). Roadkill restored!

Perhaps now we can view Jesus' death on Calvary as it really was: intentional payment to restore the roadkill of our sin—God's great act of love to make us eternally alive.

Prayer

Dear Jesus, we are sorry that we willfully wander from Your path. Forgive us and revive us through Your Holy Spirit so we might glorify You in our lives each day. Thank You for making us alive forever. In Your holy name we pray. Amen.

For further reading ... Luke 23:26–49

The Black and White Slowdown

Do you want to be free from fear of the one in authority? Then do what is right and he will commend you. Romans 13:3

There's a police car at the side of the road. The "foot-to-the-brake" syndrome kicks in. The universal guilt reflex is exercised, even though you have done nothing wrong. A sigh of relief escapes after you have passed it and it doesn't pull out.

Or perhaps you look into the rearview mirror and see the red-and-blue light bar across the top of a black-and-white car. Immediately you check the speedometer as a lump grows in your stomach and your palms begin to sweat. Again, it's the "police-car-following-me" feeling. Inside you ask, "What have I done now?"

Do you have that same queasy feeling when you catch a glimpse of God's unchangeable Law? Especially when you find yourself consistently breaking one of His commandments? That's what God's Law is for. It slows us down and makes us realize that our lives are not in sync with His.

St. Paul asks, "Do you want to be free from fear of the one in authority?" Most people would rejoice at being freed from authority. No one likes the pressure of being watched and evaluated. But Paul's answer to his own question doesn't give the relief many are seeking. Paul says "Then do what is right."

Doing what is right is exactly what we have trouble with. We try, but we are constantly speeding, making illegal turns, and traveling on the wrong side of the road. Our guilt causes us to hit the brakes and to keep looking into the

rearview mirror, wondering when we will be caught.

Good news! God *has* caught us; He caught us at our Baptism. We no longer need to feel guilty. We are forgiven through Jesus. We have been baptized into Christ's blameless record by God's amazing grace. Finding us completely in the wrong, He wrote out a traffic ticket with our name on it, but then added, "Paid in full by Jesus Christ!" Now, as forgiven, redeemed spiritual motorists, God gives us His commandments as signs of love to guide us along our journey.

Amazing! A black-and-white vehicle that slows you down on the road and a set of black-and-white commandments from God that does the same thing on your way to heaven.

Slow down when you see God in all of His holiness. Rejoice in the assurance of His constant presence in Your life.

Prayer

Thank You, O Lord God, for applying the Law to us so we might recognize our sin and flee to You for mercy. Forgive our sins, even those that cause us to doubt Your everlasting love. We thank and praise You for the sake of Your Son Jesus, in whose name we pray. Amen.

For further reading ... Genesis 4:1–16

That Lying Gas Gauge

"Peace, peace," they say, when there is no peace. Jeremiah 6:14

We live in a remarkable technological age. Advancements in electronics, communication, and medicine come so fast that it's hard to keep up. That's why I'm puzzled as to why auto manufacturers cannot make a gas gauge that tells the truth.

The one I currently put up with remains absolutely still on "F" for 100 miles. Then it suddenly comes to life as just a few miles pass by. If I were to rely solely on this faulty equipment, I would find the tank empty without a gas station in sight. I have learned to adjust and know that when the gauge says ½, we really have about ¼ of a tank left.

Is that what has happened to people today? Have we adjusted to the wicked world's lies about human nature and redemption? From the New Age corner we hear that there is some good in everyone and that to be successful that good must be nurtured and used. But in Isaiah 64:6 it says, "All of us have become like one who is unclean, and all our righteous acts are like filthy rags." Whose gauge are we to believe?

Political leaders tell us that society's ills can be corrected with just a little more money. "Eliminate poverty," they say, "and you will also eliminate crime." Whatever the human problem, they conclude that throwing money at it will get rid of it. But in the Bible God tells us that sin is the real problem and that His Son, not money, lived and died to eliminate it.

Like the gas gauge on my car, the world's gauge is not reliable. It changes its measure of right and wrong as often as most of us change socks. As in Jeremiah's time, false prophets today cry out, "Peace in our time," while all around us people and nations are at each others' throats.

We have lived so long in the garbage can of sin that we have gotten used to its smell. Hatred, violence, sexual lawlessness, and greed have polluted our spiritual atmosphere to such a degree that most of us have become numb to their presence. It's as if we become uneasy when we can't see the air we breathe. We become uncomfortable in a truly godly environment.

The world is never going to give you a gauge for godly living because it is sinful and doesn't have a moral foundation on which to stand. The message of the world would have you relying on a gauge that God tells us is empty. The only accurate gauge you will ever have is God's Word, which tells us definitively and consistently that "[Our] help comes from the LORD" (Psalm 121:2).

Prayer

Almighty God, forgive us for the many times we have believed the world's lies and dismissed Your clear truth. Enabled through Your Spirit, open our eyes to see all that You do for us each day. Make us bold to stand up and speak up when Your Word is assailed. We ask this according to Your will and for Jesus' sake. Amen.

For further reading ... Jeremiah 6:1–15

The Repair Shop

He who began a good work in you will carry it on to completion until the day of Christ Jesus. Philippians 1:6

Taking your car into a repair shop can be very frustrating. First, your vehicle has a problem and you don't know what it is or you can't fix it yourself. On top of this, you have heard about repair shops and how dishonest some can be. Some make you pay for work you don't really need. You don't have any guarantee that they will complete the work when they say they will, so you're inconvenienced by not having your car. Finally, and this is the part that hurts, you never know exactly how much the repairs will cost.

I'm afraid some people look at God in the same way. Many are taught that they are supposed to call on God when they have trouble in their lives. But some of these people approach God much like they would a mechanic: they go to Him to fix problems they can't understand or repair on their own. But they aren't exactly sure that God will really solve their problems.

"Lord, I'm sick and I want to be better. By tomorrow morning, please? And I promise I'll be at church on Sunday."

"God, I'm a little short this month—too many unexpected bills. How about a little advance on next month? I'll need it by the end of the day. And, oh yes, if I have enough left over, You'll get a little extra in the offering on Sunday."

God can and does repair broken lives, be they major or minor repairs. But His repair shop is different from what many expect. Paul described it this way, "He who began a good work in you will carry it on to completion until the day of Christ Jesus" (Philippians 1:6).

His repair service is a work that God began in you at your Baptism. Day by day, the Chief Mechanic—the Holy Spirit—hammers out the dents, recharges the battery, tunes the engine, and even fixes problems we're not aware of. The Lord is constantly working His will through us, although sometimes we aren't able to see or understand it.

The work God continually performs in our life comes with a price—a price we cannot even come close to paying. What a surprise when we see that our bill has already been paid in full—

by Jesus Christ, the proprietor Himself. And we note that what is not on the bill is grease, but blood—Christ's blood, shed for us.

When will God's work in us be done? God hasn't said. He alone knows how much more there is to do and how much more time it will take. All He says is, "Be ready!"

Prayer

Dear Lord and Savior, thank You for knowing more about what I really need than I do. Thank You for repairing my sin-damaged life. Assure me daily of Your eternal guarantee, that Your Spirit may guide my life and give me confidence in Your work. Thank You, O Lord, for allowing me to speak to You always. Amen.

For further reading ... Romans 8:28–39

Driver's Ed

Watch your life and doctrine closely. Persevere in them, because if you do, you will save both yourself and your hearers. 1 Timothy 4:16

What is your reaction when you see a car bearing the sign "Student Driver?" I suppose the first thought is automatic: "Get as far away as possible; You don't know what strange maneuvers that car will perform." Maybe you wistfully recall the days when you learned to drive. The mixed emotions come flooding back—white-knuckle terror combined with sheer excitement. Perhaps your reaction is unbridled resentment: "Here we are training another wild teenage driver. Hide the women and children, for no street will be safe again."

Timothy, St. Paul's understudy, probably felt a lot like the new driver in the driver's ed car. He was just beginning his journey as a minister of Christ. The words of Paul from 1 Timothy 4:16 sound as if they could have come from the passenger seat as young Timothy gripped the wheel of his new role with white-knuckled apprehension.

"Watch your life and doctrine closely," cautioned Paul. In our analogy he might have said, "Keep your eyes on the road while remembering all the Rules of the Road." God tells us the same thing in His Word. "Watch where you are going and keep a sharp lookout for spiritual danger. Be aware of what you believe. You can be sure that Satan is ahead of you putting up confusing, false, and misleading signs. He started this business in the Garden of Eden with our first parents and he is still at it."

Driving a Christian life these days requires that you look ahead, behind, and beside you. You must know your drivers' manual—the Bible—to be prepared for the predicaments that loom on all sides.

Paul told Timothy, "Persevere in [life and doctrine], because if you do, you will save both yourself and your hearers." Timothy was not alone in his journey and neither are we. Timothy was entrusted with the members of his congregation, just as we are entrusted with the members of our family, our friends, and fellow members of our congregation. Our life-driving skills, or our lack of them, have a profound effect on others. How we live, what we say, where we go, and what we do serve as a witness of our faith to everyone who knows us. By the power of the Holy Spirit working through us, we can help lead others into God's loving arms.

Our life is not ours. It belongs to the Father who paid an outrageous price for it. Keeping the Manual close by, we drive on through life, learning and growing in the confidence that is ours through Christ.

Prayer

Dear Father, thank You for giving us the opportunity to live our lives for You. We know how much this cost You; how painful it was for You to give up the life of Your Son for our salvation. Send Your Holy Spirit to strengthen us. Keep us close to You in every situation. Bring us safely to our journey's end, according to Your will, and for Jesus' sake. Amen.

For further reading ... 1 Timothy 4:1–16

The Car Wash

And now what are you waiting for? Get up, be baptized and wash your sins away, calling on His name. Acts 22:16

You might have a difficult time identifying the story from which this text is taken. Actually it is from a story within a story. When St. Paul spoke these words, he was within an inch of his life. He had just been rescued from an angry mob, but here he addresses the crowd, telling them how he was changed from an enemy of Christ. He refers to his own conversion experience and uses the words of Ananias. "Get up, be baptized and wash your sins away, calling on His name" (Acts 22:16).

Paul was telling the angry crowd how he came to faith. But before we pin a gold star on Paul's tunic for making the right choice, we need to realize that Paul didn't *choose* at all. In 1 Corinthians 6:9–11, Paul wrote of the marvelous turn-around of the Corinthian Christians. "But you were washed, you were sanctified, you were justified in the name of the Lord Jesus Christ and by the Spirit of our God."

Both of these clean-ups sound like modern-day car washes. It's not the driveway variety, where you handle the hose, the bucket, the sponge, and the chamois. Nor is it the neighborhood car wash, where you insert a pocketful of coins, pick up the magic wand, brace yourself, and then hang on for dear life as the wand spews out suds, water, and wax.

No, this is the automated affair. You press a button, roll up the windows, shift into neutral, sit back, and watch the suds, the gale-force deluge, followed by hurricane-style wind, which pushes the water along in shiny beads. You are magically carried along, safe and snug within your car. Now that is being baptized.

We don't wash away our sins. Instead, we are like the car in the automatic car wash. God washes us. He does all the work. He snatched Paul on his way to Damascus, drove him to his knees, doused him with His saving grace, and then blew him dry with His Spirit. This was not Paul's intention, just as your car does not decide to drive itself into the car wash. It would be more accurate to say that God cleans us up in His "people wash" while we are still in reverse.

Paul emerged a changed person despite himself. He was washed, sanctified, and justified by God. God did the same for you in your Baptism. With water and the Word, your soul was completely transformed. You were born again into Christ's redeeming grace and will now live forever as God's special child. It may not look very exciting, but your soul is having the time of its life.

Prayer

Dear Lord Jesus, thank You for covering me with the waters of Baptism. Send Your Spirit to cleanse my mind and heart today. To God alone be the glory forever and ever. In Your holy name. Amen.

For further reading ... Acts 9:1–19

Road Rage

Put on the full armor of God so that you can take your stand against the devil's schemes.
Ephesians 6:11

Recently, two men were accused of murder following an incident on a freeway on-ramp. The victim, apparently, was too slow as he got on the freeway. Two men in a vehicle behind the victim threw coffee at him as they passed. The two vehicles then left the freeway at the next exit. All three men got out of their cars and started a shoving match. The victim fell beneath the wheels of a passing truck.

This scenario, unfortunately, is duplicated in various ways throughout our country. Impatience, dangerous driving, and nastiness result in revenge, obscene gestures, and even death. All of this because of the desire to "get even." Road rage is our human nature taking control of the steering wheel and the gas pedal.

There is no question as to the origin of road rage. Satan was the first to take revenge. Ever since he was thrown out of heaven, the devil has been taking revenge on God by leading His children away from Him. He doesn't care about human beings, he cares only about hurting God. For whatever reason, he was thrown out of heaven and is even now trying to get revenge by blind-siding God's crown of creation—us.

But we need not fear. God, in His infinite wisdom and love, put an end to this wanton assault on humankind. His Son, Jesus Christ, stepped out of heaven and onto Satan's turf. There, once and for all, Jesus crushed Satan's head. Satan lies by the side of the road, still writhing, but powerless. God's rage against sin was executed on His own Son for our sake. We started the brawl, but God finished it.

The passage from Ephesians 6:11 is well known for what follows: a description of the spiritual armor God gives us to fight off Satan's anger. What is often overlooked is the purpose for the armor: "so that you can take your stand against the devil's schemes." Yes, although Satan is powerless, he still schemes. He is the one who tailgates us with accusations of guilt, swerves in and out of our lives with temptations—all in an effort to discourage us along our journey to heaven. Here is the perfect time for road rage; our version of divine wrath at sin and Satan.

We must resist sin and remember that God forgives us for all the times we do sin. Jesus took care of everyone's sin on the cross of Calvary. He endured the punishment we deserved and gave up His own life to lead us to eternal glory. As forgiven and redeemed children of God, He equips us to stand firm against the road rage attacks of the devil.

Getting even with those who commit sin against us is not in God's plan. God took care of "getting even" on Calvary. Our rage is to be against Satan who still wiggles in and out of our lives. When sin creeps its way into your life, you can confront Satan with the Word and so consign him to the wheels of God's wrath. Now that is justifiable road rage.

Prayer

Gracious Lord Jesus, forgive the many times we have sought to get even with others. Make us aware of Satan and his evil schemes, and give us strength to persevere. Grant that the Holy Spirit would help us use the armor given to us at our Baptism, so we may stand with Your saints in the Church militant. In Your name we pray. Amen.

For further reading ... Genesis 3:1–24

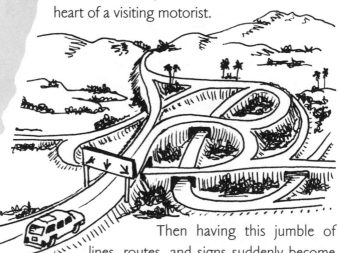

The Interchange

And we know that in all things God works for the good of those who love Him, who have been called according to His purpose. Romans 8:28

A detailed map of a freeway interchange is a truly frightening sight. In two dimensions, the knotted threads of roads, connectors, on-ramps, and exits strike fear into the heart of a visiting motorist.

Then having this jumble of lines, routes, and signs suddenly become three-dimensional is truly a nightmare. Add the speed one must travel, as well as the split-second decisions that must be made, and you have a recipe for cold sweats.

Even if you are familiar with the interchange and know which lanes lead to which exits or on ramps, you still need to worry about those who have no idea where they are going. Freeway interchanges are dreaded by all.

The way life is going these days bears a strong resemblance to an interchange. Individuals hold not one job, but two or even three. Many people have not one family, but blended families. Add concerns over debts, budgets, income, and unexpected expenses, and life becomes a confusing interchange, often leading individuals to frustration and sometimes despair.

God knows and controls all things. Notice St. Paul's words in Romans 8:28: "In all things God works... ." Nothing here about sweaty palms or fearful glances at confusing signs. "God works... ." It is God who sorts out the rat's nest of options, leading to a conclusion that is pleasing to Him, and ultimately best for us. God doesn't only work, He works for our good.

However, there is one more thing to note in this verse: "God works for the good of those who love Him, who have been called according to His purpose." This marvelous miracle of untanglement is a promise to those whom God has made His own through Baptism. As a result of His saving grace, God's children are dedicated to living their lives to His service. While they too get caught up in the mad dash around life's interchanges, they trust that a missed exit or wrong lane will be sorted out by their loving Father in heaven. The detailed map of their own freeway interchanges gets sorted out through the cross of Jesus.

Life has confusing interchanges, but God in Christ has traveled them already and bids you now to lean back and leave the driving to Him.

Prayer

Dear heavenly Father, we know how terrifying all the choices and options in life can be. We are constantly faced with decisions that seem life-changing. Speak to us through Your Word and lead us to decisions that will bring glory to You. We ask this, knowing that You answer our prayers for Jesus' sake. Amen.

For further reading ... Genesis 50:15–26

Drive-Thrus

Whenever you eat this bread and drink this cup, you proclaim the Lord's death until He comes.
1 Corinthians 11:26

We used to "drive-in," now we "drive-thru." We used to receive our hamburger on a window tray, now it comes in a sack via a seemingly unattached hand that first takes our money. We used to be served by a cheery carhop, but now we speak into a microphone. Once in awhile we actually hear a hurried, "Have a nice day."

As time has zipped by, so have we. We always seem to be in a hurry. Where we used to pause long enough to be "in," now we are so hurried we have time only for a "through."

Could we not say the same thing about our attendance at the Lord's Table? Communing with our Lord and with one another ought not be a "drive-in" or a "drive-thru." Why are we in such a hurry to get away from the Lord's Table?

Perhaps we inwardly groan when we see the Communion vessels set up on the altar. We had forgotten which Sunday or which service it was. We think, *Of course the service will last longer now. Why, then, must we sing so many verses of the hymns, and why can't the pastor shorten the sermon a bit?*

Now comes St. Paul with some advice for the almost out-of-control Corinthians. He tells them in Chapter 11 that he most certainly will not praise them for their slovenly table manners. Then he adds for them and for us, "When you eat and drink at the Lord's Table, you are preaching a visual sermon on what the Lord Jesus did for you and others."

This visual sermon is the most powerful message of man's sin and God's grace ever spoken. Why, then, are we in such a hurry to finish this sermon? Perhaps we need some extra time at the Lord's Table to hear within our soul how much we need this precious food.

Holy Communion is a means of grace. Through the body and blood Christ comes to us and the Holy Spirit strengthens our faith and forgives our sins. In Holy Communion, we are living out the wonderful message of sinful man's deliverance by the grace of God. This is a message given to you, to others, and to the whole world. Our receiving

His own body and blood is the
most powerful message of man's
sin and God's grace ever spoken.
It is a message to you, to others,
and ultimately to the world.

Jesus Christ did not quickly drive
through our world. He stopped and
prepared a heavenly banquet. Now He
patiently asks us to dine with Him. What
an honor! What a privilege! It deserves
much more than a hurried nibble and a
quick exit. In heaven we will never be "thru,"
but always "in!"

Prayer

Dear Lord Jesus, thank You for inviting us to
Your banquet—the one you begin on earth and
continue into eternity. Forgive us for the times we
are in too much of a hurry to fully appreciate what
You give us. Slow us down and enable us to savor
the love and forgiveness Your Spirit delivers in Baptism,
Holy Communion, and through Your Word. In Your
name we pray. Amen.

For further reading ... 1 Corinthians 11:17–23

Sigalert!

Even from your own number men will arise and distort the truth in order to draw away disciples after them. So be on your guard! Remember that for three years I never stopped warning each of you night and day with tears. Acts 20:30-31

Sigalert is a term unique to the Los Angeles area. The highly developed freeway system and the highly congested traffic that resulted necessitated the sigalert. When an accident occurs on any LA freeway, a sigalert will notify motorists of the accident so they can take an alternate route. This warning system is broadcast on all the major radio stations. It is therefore standard practice in LA to drive with the radio on so you can hear a sigalert. Warnings are also posted on electronic message boards that dot most of the major freeways.

As you read of Paul's adventures in the book of Acts and in his letters, you discover that he was constantly issuing sigalerts. In today's passage from Acts, Paul was alerting Christians to the fact that there were some among them who were leading them astray. In the case of our text, it was a sigalert concerning former followers of Christ who were leading unsuspecting Christians off "The Way" and into eternal destruction.

These former believers apparently did not have their radios on. Or if they did, they weren't listening. They didn't heed the warnings from God's Word, nor were they able to discern lies from the truth.

We are in the same situation today as we see one-time Christians driving blindly into spiritual confusion, unaware of God's sigalert. Others are so engrossed in their own pursuits rather than God's, that they suddenly find themselves stuck in spiritual gridlock. And others, also not paying attention, rear-end fellow travelers causing a sigalert of their own!

How distressing it must be to our Lord Jesus to see us playing bumper cars with our lives. How discouraging for Jesus to see His cross ignored. It was He who erected a message board for all to see on Mt. Calvary, only to have it ignored.

Through St. Paul, God pleads with us to be watchful, to be on guard, and to drive defensively. He urges us to pay close attention to God's sigalert provided in His Word. Through God's Word we are alerted to danger and directed to safety in the cross of Christ.

Prayer

Dear heavenly Father, we thank You for warning us through Your Word of all the dangers around us. Keep us alert to both physical and spiritual dangers that could snatch us away from Your loving arms. Be our Guard and Defender into eternity. In Jesus' name we pray. Amen.

For further reading ... Deuteronomy 30:11–20

The Car Salesman

**Always be prepared to give
an answer to everyone who
asks you to give the reason
for the hope that you have.
1 Peter 3:15**

Many of us hang our heads in shame
when the topic of personal witnessing comes
up. We know how tough it is to speak to others about Jesus Christ. We can recall many
times when a golden opportunity has slipped by.

Perhaps an example of one of our least
favorite meetings might help us with this problem.
That meeting is with the car salesman. Whether the
vehicle in question is new or used makes no difference. Such a confrontation is still no joy. Sooner or
later we find ourselves in earnest conversation
with a glib, overly friendly master of the sales
pitch.

We slowly get pulled in by the car salesman who extols the virtues of the car in which we are interested. He smoothly shifts into the details of horsepower, ABS, four-wheel drive, automatic transmission, etc. Then, when we find ourselves in the infamous little office, we become intimidated by the numerous award plaques on the wall. Then it's time to receive the barrage of financial information we thought we had mastered beforehand. Finally, as he asks if we want to drive this little beauty home today, we succumb to the pressure. We have been conquered by a master of the deal, trapped by his extreme abilities and our weak defenses.

This is not what St. Peter had in mind when he told his readers to always be ready to answer those who inquire about faith. Unbelievers have certainly never been brought to faith by slick arguments, skillfully applied by masters of the sales pitch.

Even so, the car salesman can teach us an important lesson about enthusiasm. Chances are he would get excited over any jalopy on the lot. Just show him a live prospect and he's "on." In the same way, unbelievers are often more drawn in by our enthusiasm for the Savior than by our words alone.

Without even quoting John 3:16, we can give evidence for our hope of eternity. Complaining, dour-faced critics of everyone and everything do not paint a picture of hope. But because with Him, we also have all things (Romans 8:32), we can report on half-full glasses instead of half-empty. We can be obvious positives in a negative world. How easy it becomes to shift toward a reference to Jesus Christ, who makes all of our hope possible.

Car salesmen will never sell cars if they talk only about defects. In the same way, Christians will never win over curious non-Christians if all we talk about is doom and gloom. Salvation through Christ is the most positive news ever. And the best part is that we aren't *selling* anything. God is giving it away!

Prayer

Dear heavenly Father, we praise and thank You for the gift of Your grace. Help us to approach others with joy and confidence in Your Spirit, knowing that You will supply the words we need. Fill us with the same enthusiasm that sought us and saved us from sin, death, and the power of the devil. In the name of our Savior we pray. Amen.

For further reading ... Philippians 1:12–26

Road Construction Ahead

ROAD CONSTRUCTION NEXT 453 MI

A bruised reed He will not break, and a smoldering wick He will not snuff out. Isaiah 42:3

On days when we drive smoothly along on a newly improved highway, we rarely think of road construction. The frustration of being confined to a single lane for endless miles is nowhere in sight. The flag person who held back the impatient line of traffic is forgotten. As we breeze contentedly along, we forget the rough and rutted pavement of that old, unimproved road.

Each mile of smooth driving is the result of a lengthy and costly construction job. Likewise, people are in various stages of construction. Young or old, we are all under construction.

All construction projects require patience. Yet, many times, those in charge fail to see progress and are likely to throw up their hands in frustration, saying, "I give up. This (fill blank) is beyond help." Then what happens to the project? Does it end up half-finished?

Thankfully, God didn't give up when He was faced with the ultimate construction project—us. Rather, He waded right in to our sin-fouled world, putting the tremendous burden of sin removal onto His only Son, Jesus Christ. He took the disgusting load of our sin to the cross. And talk about patience! He stuck with the project even when the people He came to save turned against Him. He stuck it out until the job was finished and defeat over sin was in the bag. Then He cried out for all the world to hear, "The job is finished."

Our heavenly Father begins His reconstruction project in our lives at Baptism. God the Holy Spirit enters our hearts through water and the Word and creates faith in Jesus Christ within us. God the Holy Spirit is in charge as He demolishes our self-pride and builds up our new life in Christ. And patience is His by-word. Isaiah says it well, "A bruised reed He will not break, and a smoldering wick He will not snuff out."

God the Spirit attends to the needs of lots of "bruised reeds." We complain, we vacillate, we fail, and He props us up. The flame of our faith flickers, sometimes appearing only as a wisp of smoke. Yet with patience and love, He fans us back to life with the life-giving breath of His Word. And lest we grow impatient with His progress, remember that this construction project will not be completed until we arrive at heaven's gate.

Our fellow Christians are also under construction. Therefore when we meet others, let us not grow weary with the Spirit's progress in them. Let us not lose patience as they stumble, bend, or flicker. Just as God is not yet finished with us, He has not finished His work in others. Just observe the construction signs and avoid impeding the Spirit's progress. In God's good time, all of us will be complete—on time, but way over budget!

Prayer

O Holy Spirit, You who gave us new life in Baptism, we thank You for Your patience in restoring us to the image of God. We pray that we may not hinder Your work with our selfish desires and hard hearts. Make us receptive to Your Word of reconciliation and eager to move ahead in our new life. We ask these things as Jesus has taught us. Amen.

For further reading ... Galatians 3:26–4:7

The Junkyard

Holding on to faith and a good conscience. Some have rejected these and so have shipwrecked their faith. 1 Timothy 1:19

We try to hide them behind groves of trees and shrubs. In urban areas they are stashed away behind fences. But we can never really make a junkyard disappear.

Piled in row after row, with hoods agape and windows gone, are the mortal remains of cars that once were the joys of proud owners. What stories these rusting hulks could tell. Tales of family trips, exciting excursions, and lazy, carefree drives. Eventually the car arrives at this place of outcasts, a place where car parts are cannibalized, leaving a vacant, empty shell. In the end, the empty body is crushed into a shapeless mass and destined for the smelter.

When St. Paul described those who had violated their consciences to Timothy, he used a story of a shipwreck. But whether it is a shipwreck disintegrating under the relentless pounding of the surf or a junkyard rusting away under heat, rain, and wind; both represent the story of disaster.

Paul advised Timothy to cling tightly to his faith in Christ. He was to grip the wheel of his faith lest he lose control of life and run off the road into ruin. It doesn't take long to lose the grip of faith. A moment of distraction or a misjudged turn into the pit of sin could have led Timothy to a fatal shipwreck and eternal disintegration. The same holds true for us today. Distraction from Christ's life within can lead to a fatal smash-up and a future in the junkyard.

Paul wrote that many former believers ended in ruin because they violated their consciences. Ignoring our consciences is similar to ignoring the warning lights on our dashboard. Overheating, an alternator that won't charge, and low oil pressure can land our vehicle in the junkyard as surely as a car wreck.

We thank our Lord for giving us a conscience to alert us to our sinful urges and tendencies. We also thank God that He sent His only Son to earn forgiveness for all the sins we commit despite the warnings from our conscience. Although Satan is always lurking, waiting for an opportunity to haul you into the junkyard, you don't have to worry. The faith that the Holy Spirit planted in your heart at Baptism will keep you away fom the junkyard, safely on the road to heaven.

Prayer

O Lord Jesus, send Your Spirit to help us negotiate the twists and turns of life. Keep our eyes on You and our ears tuned to the warning signals of sin. Keep our consciences charged with Your Spirit that we may live our lives as testimonies to Your grace. In Your name we pray. Amen.

For further reading ... 1 Timothy 6:11–21

Air Conditioning

The LORD God formed the man from the dust of the ground and breathed into his nostrils the Breath of Life, and the man became a living being.
Genesis 2:7

Physics tells us that rolling up car windows on even a moderately warm day will cause the car's interior to heat up. That is why the invention of air conditioning was such a blessing. Thankfully, the wet towels draped in partially open windows as well as the window coolers loaded with ice are gone.

Air conditioning has come a long way in efficiency and comfort. But it pales in comparison to the "air conditioning" God uses. We read about God's special air in Genesis. He created the world and everything in it. Along with all of the other perfect creations, and as the very peak of His creative work, God created humans. The second chapter of Genesis says, "And [God] breathed into [man's] nostrils the Breath of Life... ."

God's breath gave life to humankind. This same Breath of God—the Holy Spirit—breathed life into the Church on Pentecost. Acts chapter two says, "Suddenly a sound like the blowing of a violent wind came from heaven and filled the whole house where they were sitting ... All of them were filled with the Holy Spirit ..." (Acts 2:2–4).

God the Spirit gives life to individuals and to the Church. He fills us with new life in Christ at our Baptism. It is He who each day ventilates our otherwise stagnant lives with the cooling power of His gifts. He revives our wilted spirits with the refreshing breeze of the Gospel. And it is He who causes good works to flow through our lives toward others.

Our automobiles with their sophisticated climate controls, instant recognition of temperature differences, and air filters, will never compare to God's "air conditioning." Thank Him daily for

sending His ever-present cooling breath into our overheated lives. As we roll up the windows of our senses, shutting out the world's clamor, we can almost hear the soft whisper of God's breath through His Word, cooling and soothing our spirits.

Prayer

O, Holy Spirit, breathe Your life-giving breath into my life. Fill me with the blessings Jesus promises: life, forgiveness, salvation, and eternal joy. Thank You for daily refreshing me through Your Word. Continue to breathe Your holy breath of life on me until I join You, the Father, and the Son forever in eternity. Amen.

For further reading ... John 14:15–31

Home at Last!

For here we do not have an enduring city, but we are looking for the city that is to come. Hebrews 13:14

As we began our journey of travel metaphors, we discovered that Jesus Christ is the ultimate Rest Stop we all need each day to revive our spirits and forgive our sins. But let's turn our attention to general rest stops along the way.

As pleasant and necessary as rest stops are, they are not our ultimate destination. While it might be interesting to read all of the public notices on the bulletin board and dine at each of the picnic tables on the lawn, the rest stop was never meant to be more than a mere stop. In the words of the author of Hebrews, "Here we do not have an enduring city."

Yet many people, including sincere Christians, live their lives as though the rest area is the end all, be all. Their energies are spent on

pursuits that are anchored only on this earth. Wealth, prestige, power, friends, and possessions are as permanent as the hurried glimpses we have from the car's rear window. Even many Christians busy themselves in church matters that also pass in the view of the rear window as time hurtles on. The budget, the annual mother-daughter banquet, the new roof, and a lighted church sign all have their place within the work of the church, but they are not "an enduring city."

Our final destination is "the city that is to come." In chapter 11 of Hebrews, the author said, "[Abraham] was looking forward to the city with foundations, whose architect and builder is God." This city is heaven, the Promised Land, the Holy City, or the New Jerusalem. Whatever we call it, it is our ultimate goal. Our spiritual journey began at Baptism and will end when we are parked in the courtyard of at the eternal mansion prepared by our Lord and Savior.

What are our expectations as we think about our ultimate destination? Perhaps we plan to party with all of our dearly departed relatives and friends. Or maybe the prospect of life without doctors, pills, or pain is the main objective. Some are looking forward to exploring the beauties and marvels of God's new creation. We will be able to do all of these things.

The main objective of our trip should be the same as Christ's objective. Jesus said, "Father, I want those You have given Me to be with Me where I am, and to see My glory" (John 17:24). We want to make Christ happy by fulfilling His desire that we see Him as He really is. The purpose of our trip to God's city is to spend eternity with Him and our fellow Christians.

How foolish for us to fall in love with rest stops or their meager accommodations. Rest stops are wonderful and necessary, but we shouldn't get too comfortable. Rest stops? Okay—but let's keep going. Our loving Savior and eternal mansion are waiting for us just down the road.

Prayer

Our heavenly Father, thank You for the invitation, the guidance, and the free admission into Your home. Keep us pointed in Your direction as our journey continues. Bring us, according to Your plan, to Your heavenly home where we can see You in all of Your glory. We ask these things for Jesus' sake. Amen.

For further reading ... John 14:1–14

Topical Index

Scripture Reference	Page

Topical Index

Scripture Reference	Page

Index by Scripture Reference

July 2004

To our first precious niece and her sweet husband:

Dear Betty & Ollie,

We sure missed you at the family Reunion, it was not complete without you there (and Simon). It was wonderful to see the girls' pictures and hear their aunts talk so lovingly about them. Jeremy looks exactly like Ana did when you were here 2 years ago.

It was very special to have your Mom + Dad and siblings with us here for a couple of weeks. I'm sure you'll hear all about it soon. It's hard to say goodbye again. You all just live too far away, eh!

We miss you! With Love, Tante Elisabeth and family

ps I remember well how busy life is with little ones and making a living. I pray this book will encourage you both to take time out to rest in HIM and stay on the Right Road throughout life. May God Bless your family.